PRODUCTS: FROM IDEA TO MARKET

Sports Gear

by Abby Doty

Focus Readers® Beacon

www.focusreaders.com

Copyright © 2025 by Focus Readers®, Mendota Heights, MN 55120. All rights reserved. No part of this book may be reproduced or utilized in any form or by any means without written permission from the publisher.

Focus Readers is distributed by North Star Editions:
sales@northstareditions.com | 888-417-0195

Produced for Focus Readers by Red Line Editorial.

Photographs ©: Shutterstock Images, cover, 1, 8, 11, 15; iStockphoto, 4, 6, 12, 16, 19, 20, 22, 25, 29; Darron Cummings/AP Images, 26

Library of Congress Cataloging-in-Publication Data
Names: Doty, Abby, author.
Title: Sports gear: from idea to market / by Abby Doty.
Description: Mendota Heights, MN: Focus Readers, [2025] | Series: Products: From idea to market | Includes index. | Audience: Grades 2-3
Identifiers: LCCN 2024024592 (print) | LCCN 2024024593 (ebook) | ISBN 9798889984078 (hardcover) | ISBN 9798889984351 (paperback) | ISBN 9798889984887 (pdf) | ISBN 9798889984634 (ebook)
Subjects: LCSH: Athletics--Equipment and supplies--Design and construction--Juvenile literature. | Sporting goods--Design and construction--Juvenile literature. | Sporting goods industry--Juvenile literature. | Sports sponsorship--Juvenile literature.
Classification: LCC GV745 .D68 2025 (print) | LCC GV745 (ebook) | DDC 338.4/768876--dc23/eng/20240711
LC record available at https://lccn.loc.gov/2024024592
LC ebook record available at https://lccn.loc.gov/2024024593

Printed in the United States of America
Mankato, MN
012025

About the Author

Abby Doty is a writer, editor, and booklover from Minnesota.

Table of Contents

CHAPTER 1
The Football Game 5

CHAPTER 2
Great Gear 9

THAT'S AMAZING!
New Helmets 14

CHAPTER 3
Making Sports Gear 17

CHAPTER 4
Sports Ads 23

Focus Questions • 28
Glossary • 30
To Learn More • 31
Index • 32

CHAPTER 1

The Football Game

A boy gets ready for his football game. He laces up his cleats. He puts on his shoulder pads and thigh pads. He straps on his helmet. The game begins.

Football players wear lots of gear for protection and performance.

Back plates help protect football players' lower backs.

The teams play hard until the final seconds. The boy runs down the field for a pass. He sees the football fly. He reaches his arms out and grabs it. He keeps running. Another player tackles him as he falls into the end zone. The boy hits the ground. But he is not injured. His helmet and pads keep him safe. And his team wins the game. He jumps up and celebrates.

The boy is glad that his sports gear helped him. He wonders how someone created it.

Did You Know?
The first official football game was in 1869. Helmets did not become common until the 1920s.

CHAPTER 2

Great Gear

Many companies create sports gear. Their **products** help athletes play their best. Companies often try out new ideas for gear. For example, a company may try new designs for their running shoes.

Old soccer cleats used heavy leather. New cleats often use lighter materials.

That could help athletes run with more comfort and speed.

Other times, companies try out new materials. For example, they may swap the kind of metal in their baseball bats. Lighter bats are easier to swing. Companies try similar things with sports clothing. Lightweight **jerseys** help athletes move better. And they help players stay cool.

Coming up with ideas is only the first step. Next, companies make

Tennis players need clothes with strong but light fabric.

prototypes of those ideas. Workers test out the products. Testing is different for each item. People may hit or play with balls. Machines can help with the testing as well.

▶ Companies may give gear to athletes. The players can try it out to test it.

With padding, workers test how well it absorbs hits. Machines imitate the strength of hits that happen in games. Workers check that products follow safety rules, too.

Sometimes, tests show that a product is ready. Other times, workers need to make changes. They adjust the prototype and try again. Finally, the product is perfect. The company can start making and selling it.

Did You Know?
Different sports use different kinds of helmets. Bicycle helmets protect the head from falls. Football helmets protect the head from contact with other players and the ground.

THAT'S AMAZING!

New Helmets

Football helmets have changed a lot over time. In the late 1800s, some players used animal skin. By the 1920s, most players used leather helmets. These helmets had thin padding inside.

In 1939, a major change happened. The Riddell Company of Chicago made the first plastic helmet. The plastic held its shape when hit. It had a face mask, too. That helped protect the player's face.

Helmet materials continued to get better after that. Companies started making helmets lighter. They also used stronger plastic.

 Players' heads may hit each other during games.

CHAPTER 3
Making Sports Gear

Many companies make sports gear in factories. First, workers gather the materials. Each type of gear needs something different. For example, most pads require plastic and foam.

Swim caps are made of rubber. Machines prepare and shape the caps.

17

Jerseys often use **synthetic** materials. Machines create the synthetic threads. Then they knit the threads into fabric. After that, machines cut and dye the pieces. The last step is sewing. Workers put together the full jerseys.

Hockey gloves may use synthetic fabrics, too. Gloves also include leather and foam. A single glove may have 30 different pieces. So, workers use machines to help. Machines may cut the pieces out.

 Skating costumes often include tiny details. Workers may add beads or sequins by hand.

Then workers gather all the pieces. Next, they sew the gloves together by hand.

Balls are made of many materials. For example, a basketball has rubber, thread, and leather in it.

19

 Snowboarding boots are made from many different pieces. Factory workers put them all together.

Machines press sheets of rubber together. The rubber forms the ball's shape. Workers fill the ball with air. Next, machines wrap thread around the ball. Finally, they add leather pieces and more rubber. Those parts cover the finished ball.

When gear is finally done, workers check the items. They make sure the products are not broken. They look for mistakes. Then it's time to package the items. They are ready to sell.

Did You Know?

The company Wilson makes more than 700,000 footballs every year. That's more than any other company.

CHAPTER 4

Sports Ads

When gear is ready, customers can buy it. Companies **advertise** their products. Many use **commercials**. These ads show off an item's features. The ads explain why someone should buy the gear.

Ads often show players in action.

23

For instance, a commercial may describe a cleat's strong leather. It could show soccer players performing well in the cleats.

Companies often target certain kinds of buyers. Ads may show that any person can use the gear. People who play sports for fun might like that. Other companies make expensive gear. Their ads may show skilled athletes.

Other times, companies target people living in certain areas. For

Ads for ski gear often show amazing mountain sites.

example, skis sell better in snowy places. A ski company may only show ads in those places.

Athletes may also **promote** sports gear for a company. The players may use new gear during games. Players may even appear in ads.

▷ **Company logos may appear on different parts of teams' jerseys.**

Fans or other athletes see those **sponsorships**. They may want to be like the players in the ads. They decide to buy the gear.

In some cases, companies sponsor entire teams. A company supplies the team with gear. The gear shows the company's name. Players and fans see the products when they play. That helps the company sell more.

Did You Know?

Athletes can make a lot of money from sponsorships. Basketball star LeBron James partners with Nike. He earns about $32 million a year from it.

Focus Questions

Write your answers on a separate piece of paper.

1. Write a few sentences explaining the main ideas of Chapter 2.

2. If you could improve one piece of sports gear, what would it be? Why?

3. What kind of hits do bicycle helmets best protect the head from?
    - A. tackles
    - B. running
    - C. falls

4. Why would sports gear need to meet safety rules?
    - A. Athletes can get hurt using unsafe gear.
    - B. Athletes can easily lose unsafe gear.
    - C. Athletes can get tired using unsafe gear.

5. What does **injured** mean in this book?

*The boy hits the ground. But he is not **injured**. His helmet and pads keep him safe.*

    A. tall
    B. hurt
    C. fast

6. What does **adjust** mean in this book?

*Other times, workers need to make changes. They **adjust** the prototype and try again.*

    A. to keep something the same
    B. to fix something
    C. to sell something

Answer key on page 32.

Glossary

advertise

To make messages or videos about a product so customers want to buy it.

commercials

Messages or videos to sell a product. They appear during other programs.

jerseys

Shirts that athletes wear.

products

Items that are for sale.

promote

To show a product and explain why people should buy it.

prototypes

Early forms of something, usually for testing.

sponsorships

When companies pay people to promote their product.

synthetic

Made by people, not by nature.

To Learn More

BOOKS

Downs, Kieran. *LeBron James*. Minneapolis: Bellwether Media, 2023.

Green, Sara. *Nike*. Minneapolis: Bellwether Media, 2024.

Respicio, Mae. *The Story of Bicycles*. North Mankato, MN: Capstone Publishing, 2024.

NOTE TO EDUCATORS

Visit **www.focusreaders.com** to find lesson plans, activities, links, and other resources related to this title.

Index

A
advertising, 23–26

B
balls, 11, 19–21
basketball, 19–21, 27

C
cleats, 5, 24
commercials, 23–24

F
factories, 17–21
football, 5–7, 13, 14, 21

H
helmets, 5, 7, 13, 14

J
James, LeBron, 27
jerseys, 10, 18

M
machines, 11–12, 18, 20
materials, 10, 14, 17–19

N
Nike, 27

P
pads, 5, 7, 12, 14, 17
products, 9, 11–13, 21, 23, 27
prototypes, 11, 13

R
running shoes, 9–10

S
skis, 25
sponsorships, 26–27
synthetic materials, 18

T
testing, 11–13

Answer Key: 1. Answers will vary; 2. Answers will vary; 3. C; 4. A; 5. B; 6. B